Discovering Yourself *through* Journaling

Finding Confidence, Courage, and Purpose in Your Life

JOAN M. BLAKE

Key to Life
PUBLISHING COMPANY

Copyright © 2020 by Joan M. Blake • All rights reserved.

No part of this publication may be reproduced in any form or by any means, electronic or mechanical, including photocopy, recording, or any information or retrieval system, without written permission from the author.

ISBN 978-0-9814609-8-7

Published by
Key to Life Publishing Company • P.O. Box 190971 • Boston, MA 02119
keytolifepublishingcompany.com

Unless otherwise indicated, Scriptures are taken from the Holy Bible, *New International Version*® (NIV®): Copyright ©1973, 1978, 1984, 2011 by Biblica, Inc.®, 1820 Jet Stream Drive, Colorado Springs, CO 80921. Used by permission. All rights reserved worldwide.

Scriptures taken from the *New King James Version*®: Copyright © 1982 by Thomas Nelson Bibles, P.O. Box 141000, Nashville, TN 37214. Used by permission. All rights reserved.

Scriptures taken from *The Living Bible:* Copyright © 1971 by Tyndale House Foundation. Used by permission of Tyndale House Publishers Inc., 351 Executive Drive, Carol Stream, IL 60188. All rights reserved.

Printed in the United States of America

Dedication

I dedicate this book to our son Maurice, my student, who through our discussions, has acquired wisdom and understanding of Kingdom principles and who has taught me as we journey together. I pray that God will continue to bless him with wisdom, knowledge, and understanding, and that he will impart that knowledge to others.

Acknowledgements

I am grateful for the love and support of my husband, Carl, during the writing and publication of this book. I also thank my immediate family for their continued encouragement: our two sons, Karl and Maurice, our two daughters, Leah and Emily, their spouses, and all of our grandchildren.

I am grateful to close friends, prayer partners, extended family and others, who have encouraged me over the years.

I am indebted to the women and men of Evangelical Congregational Church of Atlantic, and others, for encouraging me when I launched "The Art of Journaling" as a four-week workshop, which became the foundation for this devotional.

I praise my God, who empowers me to write inspirational books; He is the source of my strength, my peace, my joy, my shield, and the lifter of my head.
—*Psalm 3:3*

Introduction

In my work as a Spiritual Coach, listening attentively to the many issues an individual discusses with me, I have come to understand how listening, writing, thinking and speaking are interconnected. For example, when I write notes or create a graph while my mentee is sharing information, that process triggers more questions for me to ask my mentee, and the questions further spark my mentee's thinking and recollection to provide more answers. For these reasons, personal journaling is a great tool. There are other forms of journaling, such as bullet, planning, travel, gratitude journaling, and many more. These are outside the scope of this discussion, but they are worth researching if you are interested in learning about them.

Discovering Yourself through Journaling: Finding Confidence, Courage, and Purpose in Your Life, includes questions to help you reflect and write about yourself, your viewpoints, your relationships, and your past. It also suggests scripture verses for you to reflect on, which will help to further your understanding of who you are in Christ, how much God loves you, how you should live and relate to others, and what your purpose is. Your study of these passages from Scripture will cause you to love yourself, maintain confidence, improve your self-esteem, and reach out in forgiving and loving others. You will become patient with God as He molds and shapes you into a person with a renewed mind and zeal and with a purpose—to live a life of joy, peace, and hope.

I learned the importance of journaling in the early 90's when I started writing my thoughts and feelings in my journals during personal retreats or while on family vacations. During personal retreats, I would write pages and pages in my journal in the morning and then take a long walk. After dinner, I would lounge around in my room, read the Bible, and write again. While I didn't write in my journal more than once or twice per year, I was still consistent in writing. That would change eventually to writing more on a monthly basis, then weekly, then daily; I suggest that whatever you are comfortable with, do it, and be consistent.

The journal became my secret place to write about joyous times, to vent about my feelings, and to learn how I should react to every situation I faced. Most importantly, my journal became meaningful when I reviewed my entries that were written over time and realized that in some instances I did not mature, while in others, I was holding on to emotions that hindered my spiritual growth. Carl J Koch, in his book *Journalkeeping*, showed me that my journal had become a tool where I could free up my mind, have spiritual reflection, and gain wisdom and healing in the process. In reading Alexandra Johnson's book, *Leaving a Trace: The Art of Transforming a Life into Stories*, I realized that my journal entries translated, as she indicates, into a story of my life. That became even more evident when I sought my journals in order to write my first memoir, *Standing on His Promises: Finding Comfort, Hope, and Purpose in the Midst of Your Storm*.

I shared my eye-catching revelations about personal journaling in several workshops that I conducted. The first was a memoir writing class that I taught to a small group of women at a Boston branch library where we met consecutively for six weeks. I encouraged them in the use of imagery, words, color, and personality characteristics, to spark memory. Not everyone shared her personal story, but the women recorded their thoughts and feelings in their journals, had a time of reflection, and were able to heal from past hurts.

The second workshop, a short version of this book, I taught to a group of women and men at a church I was attending. Our weekly sessions included journal writing, scripture reading and application and small group discussion. Some women journaled during this class for the first time and found that writing their thoughts and feelings in their personal journals allowed them to see who they truly were. In the third instance, I used my book, *Prayer and Meditation for Teens*, to create "The Art of Journaling for Teens," a workshop where I shared journaling techniques to a group of teenagers who were eager to open up and be in touch with their real selves. In all of the workshops I offered, journaling seemed to be an interesting theme for people of all ages.

It is my joy to introduce you to *Discovering Yourself through Journaling: Finding Confidence, Courage, and Purpose in Your Life,* to allow you to freely write your thoughts and feelings so that you will better understand the areas of your life in which you may be looking for help. Writing your thoughts and feelings down, I believe, is paramount to being in touch with your subconscious, where thoughts/feelings are buried and lay dormant. I believe that when you write about your feelings, you bring them to light and you uncover the hidden things of your heart. You are able then to identify areas that have held you captive and be healed from them. On the other side of this spectrum is the ability for you to unleash the greatness that had remained hidden in you and discover who you really are.

This book can be used as a personal devotional for anyone who desperately desires to go on a journey to find and equip himself/herself biblically. While this journal tool does not replace counseling, spiritual counselors or coaches can use this tool to obtain basic information from their clients. Church leaders or organizational managers who routinely conduct training, retreats or weekly classes for their members, will find these journal exercises helpful. Additionally, this book can be used as a beginning writing course for those who are interested in pursuing writing.

I pray that *Discovering Yourself through Journaling: Finding Confidence, Courage, and Purpose in Your Life,* will help you discover who you really are, and uncover the hidden greatness in you. I trust that you will become that person who God has called you to be. His desire is for you to discover your uniqueness, find your purpose, and take your position as an ambassador for Christ.

Table of Contents

Introduction V

PART I **Discovering Yourself through Journaling** 3

WEEK 1 Explain fully how you feel: how has life been going? 4

WEEK 2 Describe a happy or sad moment in your past. 7

WEEK 3 Uncover any secret in your past. 10

WEEK 4 Think of a time when you enjoyed yourself. 13

WEEK 5 Think of an important event that's impacted your life. 16

WEEK 6 Have you been dealing with guilt, anger or unforgiveness? 19

WEEK 7 What challenges are you currently facing? 22

WEEK 8 What patterns have you noticed in your family? 24

WEEK 9 What life lessons have you learned from a mentor? 27

WEEK 10 What emotions need to be uprooted? 30

WEEK 11 What decisions have you made concerning moving or changing careers? 33

WEEK 12 What additional areas you are having challenges in? 36

Part II:	Discovering Yourself through Journaling	38
Week 13.	Discovering Who You Are.	39
Week 14.	Gathering Information from Your Past.	46
Week 15	Understanding Jesus' Purpose and Your Purpose.	53
Week 16	Breaking from Old Habits, Thoughts and Patterns	67
Week 17	Realizing that You Need a Spiritual Breakthrough	82
Week 18	Picturing Yourself as Having Accomplished Your Purpose	106
Week 19	Moving to the Next Level with God	110
Week 20	Walking with God	121
Bibliography		145
About the Author		146
Contact Information		147

Discovering Yourself through Journaling

Part One

Discovering Yourself through Journaling, Part I, gives you an opportunity to go on a 12-week journey of finding yourself through personal journaling. The objective is to provide you with questions and allow you to write freely about yourself, your viewpoints, your relationships and your past, which will help you to identify areas that have kept you captive so you can obtain the help you need. When you write freely, you bring to light what has been hidden in your subconscious, for example, your hurts and pains, the reasons for your hurts, your fears, your guilt, your anger and a multitude of issues that you face that have prevented you from discovering your talents which lay dormant inside you. This process allows you to heal, walk in your purpose, and set realistic goals to change your behavior and become the woman or man that God has called you to be.

Week 1.

Explain fully who you are; how you feel about yourself. How has your life been going?

Reflect:
Imagine if someone should ask you, "How are you today? How did you feel last week, last month or last year?" What would your answer be?

Spark your memory.
Think of how happy you were last year. What has that been like? What changed in your life to make things better or worse? Although your life-issue had worsened, what exciting things are you doing for yourself that make you feel happy? What things would you like to see changed?

Respond:
Explain fully who you are, how you feel about yourself, how others perceive you. Be honest and explain why they perceive you the way they do. Give reasons why you are bothered by the way others perceive you.

How has life been going so far for you? Simply write freely. Do not think too hard. Allow your thoughts to flow right on to the paper or the computer.

Week 2.

Describe a happy or sad moment in your past.

Reflect:
Think about a happy or sad moment in your past. How did you react to that moment?

> **Spark your memory.**
> Think about your favorite color, a birthday party your friends or family threw for you, your high school play, your piano or dance recital, your soccer tournament or your basketball tournament, mountain climbing, hiking or skiing. Think about your siblings and their relationship to you.

Respond:
How did your family and friends react to seeing you happy?

Similarly, write about a sad moment in your past. Did you experience trauma as a young person?

What happened? How did you react? How did it leave you feeling (guilty, bitter, angry, jealous, unforgiving, lonely or did you have other emotions?) Explain your reasons for feeling that way.

Week 3.

Uncover any secret in your past.

Reflect:
Think about a secret in your past that may be lingering over you and that may be responsible for your being and acting the way you do.

> ### *Spark your memory.*
> *If it's relevant for you, visualize yourself crying, someone telling you: "Do not tell anyone." When was the first time you remember feeling a sense of loneliness, fear, sadness or abandonment?*

Respond:

Has this revelation been the reason for your current response to life?

How was your relationship with your mother, dad, siblings and extended relatives, friends or strangers?

Describe your relationship with your significant other—
your husband/wife/boyfriend/girlfriend. For example,
do you have a trust issue because of your previous relationships?
Explain fully.

Week 4.

Think of a time when you enjoyed yourself.

Reflect:
Think about a period in your life that you had fun and enjoyed yourself fully.

Spark your memory.
Describe your prom night, your engagement party, your birthday party or a fun event in which you participated.

Respond:
Describe that period when you enjoyed yourself, when it occurred, where it was celebrated, and how you enjoyed yourself.

Are you still enjoying yourself? If not, why?

Week 5.

Think of an important event that has impacted your life.

Reflect:
Think of an important event that happened in your teenage years that had an important impact on your life now.

> *Spark your memory.*
>
> *Think about the death of your grandmother, grandfather, best friend or other person. Describe the type of relationship you had with them.*

Respond:
For example, did you lose an important tournament or were there other reasons that caused your parents to feel disappointed?

Did you feel abandoned having left your home early in life?

Did you experience the loss of a loved one or a best friend? What happened? How did you react to the issue then and now?

Why did you react to the issue or issues the way you did?

Week 6.

Have you been dealing with guilt, anger or unforgiveness?

Reflect:
Have you been feeling guilty for hurting someone's feelings, angry or unforgiving toward someone who had hurt your feelings?

> *Spark your memory.*
> *Your best friend said something about you that made you angry. Think about your sibling rivalry and how difficult it was to live with your siblings, and to deal with them.*

Respond:
Explain the reason(s) you feel this way. Write freely about your situation.

After describing this situation, find a solution and put your issue to rest. Explain how you will go about putting your issue to rest.

Week 7.

What challenges are you currently facing?

Reflect:
If you could, try to imagine a solution you could use for every challenge you face—what would that look like?

> *Spark your memory.*
> Think about challenges you may have such as over-eating, smoking, under-eating, procrastination, and laziness.

Respond:
Describe your current challenges.

Week 8.

What patterns have you noticed in your family?

Reflect:
Think about patterns that you have recognized in your life or have learned about in your family from generations past.

> *Spark your memory.*
> *Did past generations in your family attend college, own homes, yell at their children, not speak to their children with love, or have dysfunctional households?*

Respond:
Are you living in a rut? Do you continue to struggle in the same manner as your extended family members from generations past? How have you been struggling? (For example, have you been struggling with depression, drug and alcoholic issues, marriage issues, co-dependency and/or other issues?)

Understand that you do not have to follow or practice the things that your previous generations have done. Take the step to eradicate these challenges from your life by finding a solution to your problem.

How do you plan on solving your problem and why?

Week 9.

What life lessons have you learned from a mentor? Has anyone mentored you lately?

Reflect:
Think of the discussions you had with your friend, mentor or counselor.

> *Spark your memory.*
> *Think about what you discussed with your mentor or counselor. (For example, anger, fear, unhappiness).*

Respond:
What life solutions have you learned from your friend, mentor, or counselor?

Were you able to put these lessons into practice or are you still thinking about what to do?

What do you think you need to do now? Why?

Week 10.

What emotions need to be uprooted?

Reflect:
Think of emotions that trouble you every day.

> ### *Spark your memory.*
> Think about loneliness, fear, unforgiveness and jealousy. What strategies or plans did you utilize to deal with these difficult emotions? Take loneliness for example, did you join a group with members who had similar issues? Were you able to speak about the issues at meetings?

Respond:

What one word describes you? Why? Describe emotions that stay dormant in your mind and need to be uprooted. (For example, fear, bitterness, anger, rebellion, control, jealousy.)

Explain fully how you plan to deal with any or all of your given emotions.

Week 11.

What decisions have you made concerning moving and/or changing careers?

Reflect:
Assume that you are considering moving to another state because you are looking for a new job.

> *Spark your memory.*
> *Think about what comfort is all about. Think about what happiness looks like. Think about taking risks when you do not have friends.*

Respond:
Assume that you moved and found a job and made friends at work. You faced the fact that you would have to move to an apartment soon and would need a roommate. How do you plan to solve this problem?

Maybe you are moving to a new apartment or thinking of buying a house in the state you currently live. As you write, think about your issue and begin putting a solution into place.

Week 12.

What additional areas are you having challenges in?

Reflect:
You have arrived at the twelfth week of this journaling journey and you want a complete makeover of your life. What other areas in your life need a life-change?

> *Spark your memory.*
> *Think of unforgiveness, when you enjoyed life, think of hope, peace, longsuffering, faith and happiness.*

Respond:
List other areas in your life that need changing, and for each area, begin to write an action plan that will include short-term and long-term goals.

Discovering Yourself through Journaling

Part Two

After journaling freely for 12 weeks and discovering areas that held you captive, now you are ready for *Discovering Yourself through Journaling Part II*. Here, we introduce you to scripture verses that affirm God's unconditional love for you, your inheritance as a child of God, and the gifts and talents that God has given you. The study of these passages will cause you to love yourself, maintain confidence, improve your self-esteem, and reach out in forgiveness and love to others. You would become renewed by God's Holy Spirit as He guides you into a life of peace, hope, and joy. Your faith in God will increase as you begin to walk with God, listen, and obey his voice. You will become energized and transformed into a vessel that God will use to take the Gospel of peace to your neighbors and wherever you go.

Week 13.

Discovering Who You Are

In this study, you will learn:
- Who God says that you are, as you read, study, analyze, summarize, and respond to the following scripture verses:
    - Ephesians 1:3-6
    - Jeremiah 31:3
    - Romans 8:15-17
    - 2 Corinthians 5:17

- You will unlock new discoveries about yourself by reviewing:
    - Ephesians 1:3-6
    - Jeremiah 31:3
    - Romans 8:15-17
    - 2 Corinthians 5:17

Week 13. Discovering Who You Are
Who does God say that you are?
Read and study Ephesians 1:3-6.
> Praise be to the God and Father of our Lord Jesus Christ, who has blessed us in the heavenly realms with every spiritual blessing in Christ. For he chose us in him before the creation of the world to be holy and blameless in his sight. In love he predestined us for adoption to sonship through Jesus Christ, in accordance with his pleasure and will—to the praise of his glorious grace, which he has freely given us in the One he loves.

Notes from the *Reformation Study* Bible
The Redeemer, Christ, the object of God's love, was raised from the dead and seated at the right hand of the Father from where he governs all things. Christ's victory over death has won benefits for believers. God chooses people for a relationship with Himself. God's intention is to bring his people from spiritual death in sin to forgiveness, and lastly from all sin (Rom. 8:29-30).

Analyze:
What are the key points from Ephesians 1:3-6?

Summarize:
In your own words, explain Ephesians 1:3-6.

Read and study Jeremiah 31:3.
  The Lord appeared to us in the past, saying:
  "I have loved you with an everlasting love;
  I have drawn you with unfailing kindness."

Notes from the *Reformation Study* Bible
The Lord's love for Israel was the basis for his election of them (Deut.7:6). His everlasting character of his covenant can be viewed in (Genesis 17:7).

Analyze:
What are the key points from Jeremiah 31:3?

Summarize:
In your own words, explain Jeremiah 31:3.

Read and study Romans 8:15-17.
> The Spirit you received does not make you slaves, so that you live in fear again; rather, the Spirit you received brought about your adoption to sonship. And by him we cry, "Abba, Father." The Spirit himself testifies with our spirit that we are God's children. Now if we are children, then we are heirs—heirs of God and co-heirs with Christ, if indeed we share in his sufferings in order that we may also share in his glory.

Notes from the *Reformation Study* Bible
In addition to justification and freedom from condemnation, believers are accepted into the family of God through the Spirit and are persuaded inwardly to belong there. Abba was used by Jesus himself, for God, (Mark 14:36). This cry was an expression of sonship. In a family, all children are heirs of the father, so in Christ, we are heirs, as we share in his sufferings, the way to participating in his glory.

Analyze:
What are the key points from Romans 8:15-17?

Summarize:
In your own words, explain Romans 8:15-17.

Read and study 2 Corinthians 5:17 (NKJV).
Therefore, if anyone is in Christ, he is a new creation; old things have passed away; behold, all things have become new.

Notes from the *Reformation Study* Bible
Union with Christ summarizes our experience of redemption. Believers are elected (Eph. 1:4,11), justified (Rom. 8:1), sanctified (1 Co. 1:2), and glorified (2 Co. 3:18).

Analyze:
What are the key points from 2 Corinthians 5:17?

Summarize:
In your own words, explain 2 Corinthians 5:17.

Respond:
Using the following scripture verses, key points, and your own explanations, write a detailed summary of who you are from God's perspective.

- Ephesians 1:3-6
- Jeremiah 31:3
- Romans 8:15-17
- 2 Corinthians 5:17

In what ways have these views changed your perspective on life?

Respond:
Using the same scriptures: Ephesians 1:3-6, Jeremiah 31:3, Romans 8:15-17 and 2 Corinthians 5:17, describe something new that you have discovered about yourself that you were not aware of. Feel free to describe many new things you learned if it fits with your experience of studying the scriptures.

Week 14.

Gathering Information from Your Past

- Describe your relationship with your friends and relatives.

- Describe your relationship with your co-workers.

- Describe your relationship with people in your community, (for example, in your church, temple or synagogue.)

- Describe your relationship with your significant other (for example, your husband/wife/boyfriend/girlfriend.)

- Describe, define, and give examples of a belief system.

- Describe your belief system. A belief system causes you to feel and act a certain way.

Describe your relationships with your friends and relatives and explain how your relationships have shaped your thinking and actions.

Describe your relationships with your co-workers in the past, as well as now, and explain how your relationships have shaped your thinking and actions.

Describe your relationships with people in your community (for example, in your church/temple/synagogue.) Describe how these relationships have shaped your thinking and actions.

Describe your relationship with your significant other: your husband/wife/boyfriend/girlfriend. Describe how this relationship has shaped your thinking and actions.

Describe, define, and give examples of a belief system.
According to the *Collins English Dictionary,* the belief system of a person or society is the set of beliefs that they have about what is right and wrong and what is true and false. There are many belief systems; here are three examples of religious belief systems, taken from http://www.humanreligions.info/religions.html:

> **Agnosticism** is a form of belief, rather than a specific system. It's a belief that:
>
> 1. God, if it exists, is by nature unknowable and will always be unknowable, or,
>
> 2. that the individual being asked cannot conclude if God exists or not for lack of evidence one way or the other.
>
> **Buddhism** is a world religion founded on the belief that meditation and good living can break the cycle of reincarnation and result in enlightenment.
>
> **Christianity** is the belief that a single creator God had a Son, Jesus Christ, born to a human mother, and that Jesus' crucifixion by the Romans brings salvation.

Describe your belief system.

The belief system you embrace causes you to feel and act a certain way. Explain how your belief system has impacted your way of life including your relationships with others.

Week 15.

Knowing Jesus' Purpose

- Defining "Purpose"

- Knowing Jesus' Purpose
  Read, study, analyze, summarize, and respond to the following scripture verses to learn about Jesus' purpose.
    - Isaiah 61:1
    - John 14:6
    - John 17:2-3
    - Romans 8:34

- Knowing Your Purpose

- Do you know your purpose? Yes/No

- If you answered "Yes," describe your purpose and the plans that you have put in place to achieve your purpose.

- If you answered "No," to the previous question, what is preventing you from achieving your purpose? Discuss fully.

- If you are experiencing stumbling blocks, describe your experiences fully and explain what you need to do to overcome them.

- Are you experiencing procrastination? Describe your issue in detail and explain what you need to do to overcome this problem.

- Describe instances where you experienced low self-esteem. What do you need to do to prevent this problem from surfacing again?

- Identify other areas in your life that prevent you from achieving your purpose. What do you need to do to get back on track?

Defining "Purpose"
According to Dictionary.com, *purpose* can include an aim, intent or goal for oneself. For example, a person may have a spiritual goal of seeing himself/herself through the lens of Jesus, having a purpose of being a minister to help others. Jesus' purpose in coming to the earth was to redeem humanity from the curse of sin and death (Gal 3:13) by dying on the cross.

Knowing Jesus' Purpose
Read and study Isaiah 61:1.

> The Spirit of the Sovereign Lord is on me, because the Lord has anointed me to proclaim good news to the poor. He has sent me to bind up the brokenhearted to proclaim freedom for the captives and release from darkness for the prisoners.

Notes from the *Reformation Study* Bible
This prophecy was fulfilled in the ministry of Christ. Refer to Isaiah 11:2; 42:1; Luke 3:22; Luke 4:18-19.

Analyze:
What are the key points from Isaiah 61:1?

Summarize:
In your own words, explain Isaiah 61:1.

Read and study John 14:6.
> Jesus answered, "I am the way and the truth and the life. No one comes to the Father except through me."

Notes from the *Reformation Study* Bible
We should be God's living temples. See John 1:4. Salvation is through Christ alone. To think in other ways is misleading people and forget about his coming and redemption (Acts 4:12; Rom. 10:14, 15).

Analyze:
What are the key points from John 14:6?

Summarize:
In your own words, explain John 14:6.

Read and study John 17:2-3.
For you granted him authority over all people that he might give eternal life to all those you have given him. Now this is eternal life: that they know you, the only true God, and Jesus Christ, whom you have sent.

Notes from the *Reformation Study* Bible
Eternal life is to whom God has given him. Life consists in fellowship with God who has created us for himself; our souls are restless until we find our rest in him. Christ affirms his own deity by putting himself with the Father as the source of eternal life.

Analyze:
What are the key points from John 17:2-3?

Summarize:
In your own words, explain John 17:2-3.

Read and study Romans 8:34 (TLB).
Who then will condemn us? Will Christ? No! For he is the one who died for us and came back to life again for us and is sitting at the place of highest honor next to God, pleading for us there in heaven.

Notes from the *Reformation Study* Bible
Jesus sits at the right hand of the Father with honor and authority. He is our sin-bearer who intercedes for us (1 John 2:1) while the Holy Spirit intervenes in our hearts (1 John 2:27).

Analyze:
What are the key points from Romans 8:34?

Summarize:
In your own words, explain Romans 8:34.

Respond:
Based on the key points and your study of the following scripture verses: Isaiah 61:1, John 14:6, John 17:2-3, and Romans 8:34, explain Jesus' purpose in your own words.

Respond:
Pick one or two scripture verses from the following: Isaiah 61:1, John 14:6, John 17:2-3, and Romans 8:34, and explain the ways in which Jesus' purpose was focused on you.

Do you know your purpose?

☐ Yes   ☐ No

If you answered "Yes," describe your purpose and the plans that you have put in place to achieve your purpose.

If you answered "No," to the previous question, what is preventing you from achieving your purpose? Discuss fully.

If you are experiencing stumbling blocks, describe your experiences fully and explain what you need to do to overcome them.

Are you experiencing procrastination? Describe your issue in detail and explain what you need to do to overcome this problem.

Describe instances where you experienced low self-esteem. What do you need to do to prevent this problem from surfacing again?

Identify other areas in your life that prevent you from achieving your purpose. What do you need to do to get back on track?

Week 16.

Breaking from Old Habits, Thoughts, and Patterns

- What is your view on love?
- Explain reasons for not loving others, if you have this problem.
- In what ways does your negative behavior impact your relationships/making new friends?
- Explain your prejudices, likes, and dislikes.
- What old habits do you need to break from?
- What thoughts have you allowed to clog your mind?
- What life patterns do you need to break from?
- Read, study, analyze, summarize, and respond to the following scripture verses to learn about how to break from old life patterns:
    - Ephesians 4:1-3
    - Romans 13:9
    - Galatians 5: 19-21
    - Galatians 5: 22-26
- Write a letter to God explaining the difficulties you are experiencing and how you plan to move forward with His help.
- Confess, repent and ask God to forgive you in those areas you want to be freed from.
- Recite the prayer of salvation.

What is your view on love?

Explain the reasons for not loving others, if you have this problem.

In what ways does your negative behavior impact your relationships/ making new friends?

Explain your prejudices, likes, and dislikes.

What old habits do you need to break from (for example, gossiping, jealousy, hate, and lying)?

What thoughts have you allowed to clog your mind (for example, fear and anxiety)?

What life patterns do you need to break from (for example: living in a rut, over-spending)?

Read and study Ephesians 4:1-3 (TLB).
I beg you—I, a prisoner here in jail for serving the Lord—to live and act in a way worthy of those who have been chosen for such wonderful blessings as these. Be humble and gentle. Be patient with each other, making allowance for each other's faults because of your love. Try always to be led along together by the Holy Spirit and so be at peace with one another.

Notes from the *Reformation Study* Bible
Paul focuses on the life that a believer should live coupled with good works.

Analyze:
What are the key points from Ephesians 4:1-3?

Summarize:
In your own words, explain Ephesians 4:1-3.

Read and study Romans 13:9 (TLB).
If you love your neighbor as much as you love yourself you will not want to harm or cheat him or kill him or steal from him. And you won't sin with his wife or want what is his or do anything else the Ten Commandments say is wrong. All ten are wrapped up in this one, to love your neighbor as you love yourself.

Notes from the *Reformation Study* Bible
Love your neighbor, who is created in the image of God, like yourself. Refer to Gen. 1:26, 27; Luke 6:31.

Analyze:
What are the key points from Romans 13:9?

Summarize:
In your own words, explain Romans 13:9.

Read and study Galatians 5:19-21 (NKJV).
Now the works of the flesh are evident, which are: adultery, fornication, uncleanness, lewdness, idolatry, sorcery, hatred, contentions, jealousies, outbursts of wrath, selfish ambitions, dissensions, heresies, envy, murders, drunkenness, revelries, and the like; of which I tell you beforehand, just as I also told you in time past, that those who practice such things will not inherit the kingdom of God. When you follow the desires of your sinful nature, the results are very clear: sexual immorality, impurity, lustful pleasures, idolatry, sorcery, hostility, quarreling, jealousy, outbursts of anger, selfish ambition, dissension, division, envy, drunkenness, wild parties, and other sins like these. Let me tell you again, as I have before, that anyone living that sort of life will not inherit the Kingdom of God.

Notes from the *Reformation Study* Bible
Paul lists sins that will not qualify the sinner from entering the kingdom of God. Refer to 1 Cor. 6:9,10; Eph.5:5.

Analyze:
What are the key points from Galatians 5:19-21?

Summarize:
In your own words, explain Galatians 5:19-21.

Read and study Galatians 5:22-26.
But the fruit of the Spirit is love, joy, peace, forbearance, kindness, goodness, faithfulness, gentleness and self-control. Against such things there is no law. Those who belong to Christ Jesus have crucified the flesh with its passions and desires. Since we live by the Spirit, let us keep in step with the Spirit. Let us not become conceited, provoking and envying each other.

Notes from the *Reformation Study* Bible
Paul uses "fruit" to describe the type of behavior that the believer should exhibit. True repentance brings out ethical behavior. Refer to Matt.3:8 and Luke 3:8.

Analyze:
What are the key points from Galatians 5:22-26?

Summarize:
In your own words, explain Galatians 5:22-26.

Read and study Romans 10:9 (NKJV).
…That if you confess with your mouth the Lord Jesus and believe in your heart that God has raised Him from the dead, you will be saved.

Notes from the *Reformation Study* Bible
Paul explains that mouth confession and heart belief are bases for justification (salvation).

Analyze:
What are the key points from Romans 10:9?

Summarize:
In your own words, explain Romans 10:9.

Write a letter to God explaining the difficulties you are experiencing and how you plan to move forward with His help.

Respond:
Confess, repent and ask God to forgive you in those areas you want to be freed from.

Recite the prayer of salvation below.

Prayer of Salvation
Lord God of the Universe,
Creator of everything (Colossians 1:16),
I come to you in desperation,
desiring to have an intimate relationship with You
and to invite Jesus Christ to be my Lord and Savior (Isaiah 43:3).

I confess and repent of my sins
and ask for Your forgiveness.
I accept Jesus as my Lord and Savior,
The One who died on the cross and rose again,
paying the penalty for my sins,
so I could have salvation and eternal life (John 3:16).
I pray this in Jesus' name, Amen.

Week 17.

Realize that you need a spiritual breakthrough.

- Obtain your spiritual breakthrough by studying God's Word, praying, praising, and worshiping God.

- Read, study, analyze, summarize, and respond to the following scripture verses to learn about studying God's Word, praying, praising, and worshiping God.
    - Psalm 119:105
    - Psalm 5:2
    - Psalm 104:33
    - John 4:24

- What changes do you believe will take place when you begin praying, praising, and worshiping God?

- Confessing, Repenting, and Asking God for Forgiveness

- Read, study, analyze, summarize, and respond to the following scripture verses to learn about confessing, repenting and asking God for forgiveness:
    - 1 John 1:9
    - Matthew 6:15
    - Acts 3:19

- Renewing Your Mind
    - Definition—Changing Your Mindset

- Read, study, analyze, summarize, and respond to the following scripture verses to learn about renewing your mind:
    - Romans 12: 1-2
    - Ephesians 4: 31-32

- Establishing Faith in God

- Read, study, analyze, summarize, and respond to the following scripture verses to establish your faith in God:
    - Hebrews 11:1
    - Hebrews 10:23
    - Ephesians 2:8
    - 1 Corinthians 16:13
    - Hebrews 11:6

- Standing on God's Promises Regardless of How You Feel

- Read, study, analyze, summarize, and respond to the following scripture verses to learn about standing on God's promises:
    - Psalm 145:13
    - Joshua 23:14

Obtain your spiritual breakthrough by studying God's Word, praying, praising, and worshiping God.

Read and study Psalm 119:105 (NKJV).

Your word is a lamp to my feet
and a light to my path.

Notes from the *Reformation Study* Bible
God's revelation provides insights to guide his servants.

Analyze:
What are the key points from Psalm 119:105?

Summarize:
In your own words, explain Psalm 119:105.

Respond:
What have you gained from reading and studying the Word of God?

Read and study Psalm 5:2 (NKJV).

> Give heed to the voice of my cry,
> my King and my God,
> for to You I will pray.

Notes from the *Reformation Study* Bible
David, Israel's King, addresses God as his king.

Analyze:
What are the key points from Psalm 5:2?

Summarize:
In your own words, explain Psalm 5:2.

Read and study Psalm 104:33.
I will sing to the Lord all my life; I will sing praise to my God as long as I live.

Notes from the *Reformation Study* Bible
This verse shows that the Creator alone should be praised and worshiped.

Analyze:
What are the key points from Psalm 104:33?

Summarize:
In your own words, explain Psalm 104:33.

Read and study John 4:24.
God is spirit, and his worshipers must worship in the Spirit and in truth.

Notes from the *Reformation Study* Bible
True worship is contrasted with worship regulated by the temporary provisions of the law which separated Jews and Gentiles and restricted worship to temple worship. Now, in Christ, there is the removal of the barriers of Jews and Gentiles and worship in the Spirit and the ability of Christians to worship without the need of a temple of any kind.

Analyze:
What are the key points in John 4:24?

Summarize:
In your own words, explain John 4:24.

Respond:
What changes do you believe will take place in your life when you begin praying, praising and worshiping God?

Obtain your breakthrough by confessing, repenting, and asking God for forgiveness.

Read and study 1 John 1:9 (NKJV).
If we confess our sins, He is faithful and just to forgive us our sins and to cleanse us from all unrighteousness.

Notes from the *Reformation Study* Bible
As soon as we acknowledge our need, God forgives us by His grace and not by any acts or deeds that we offer him. The free gift of forgiveness carries with it, purification from unrighteousness.

Analyze:
What are the key points from 1 John 1:9?

Summarize:
In your own words, explain 1 John 1:9.

Read and study Matthew 6:15.
But if you do not forgive others their sins, your Father will not forgive your sins.

Notes from the *Reformation Study* Bible
Jesus was directing his sermon on the Mount to His disciples as well as to the whole church today. The sermon addressed both inward motives and outward conduct.

Analyze:
What are the key points from Matthew 6:15?

Summarize:
In your own words, explain Matthew 6:15.

Read and study Acts 3:19 (TLB).
Now change your mind and attitude to God and turn to him so he can cleanse away your sins and send you wonderful times of refreshment from the presence of the Lord.

Notes from the *Reformation Study* Bible
Peter's sermon illustrates the two sides of repentance, that is, turning aside in sorrow from sin, and turning to God in faith. The call to repentance and faith is a necessary element of the apostolic preaching. In the order of the gospel, when you repent by faith, you receive from God forgiveness and removal of sins.

Analyze:
What are the key points from Acts 3:19?

Summarize:
In your own words, explain Acts 3:19.

Respond:
In what ways can you apply 1 John 1:9, Matthew 6:15, or Acts 3:19 to your life?

Respond:
Pick a scripture verse from the following: 1 John 1:9, Matthew 6:15, and Acts 3:19, which speaks to an urgent decision you must make in your life. Discuss the issue that you need to confess. If it's unforgiveness, take time now to forgive others of their wrongdoings; confess, repent, and receive forgiveness from the Lord for that, and other issues, that you may have.

Obtain your spiritual breakthrough by renewing your mind.

Definition of Renewing Your Mind
Renewing your mind means changing your mindset and living Godly.

Read and study Romans 12:1-2.
Therefore, I urge you, brothers and sisters, in view of God's mercy, to offer your bodies as a living sacrifice, holy and pleasing to God—this is your true and proper worship. Do not conform to the pattern of this world but be transformed by the renewing of your mind. Then you will be able to test and approve what God's will is—his good, pleasing and perfect will.

Notes from the *Reformation Study* Bible
Bodies mean whole bodies both Jew and Gentiles, the body of Christ, for whom Jesus shed his blood. The Christian's mindset is to be determined and reshaped by the knowledge of the Gospel, by the power of the Spirit and the concerns of the age to come. Only by sanctification can the Christian "discern" the behavior that is God's will in each situation.

Analyze:
What are the key points from Romans 12:1-2?

Summarize:
In your own words, explain Romans 12:1-2.

Read and study Ephesians 4:31-32 (TLB).
Stop being mean, bad-tempered, and angry. Quarreling, harsh words, and dislike of others should have no place in your lives. Instead, be kind to each other, tenderhearted, forgiving one another, just as God has forgiven you because you belong to Christ.

Notes from the *Reformation Study* Bible
Apostle Paul shows how a Christian must move from their old way of life and put on a "life" in Christ.

Analyze:
What are the key points from Ephesians 4:31-32?

Summarize:
In your own words, explain Ephesians 4:31-32.

Respond:
Describe how you plan to apply Romans 12:1-2 and Ephesians 4:31-32 to your life.

Obtain your spiritual breakthrough by establishing faith in God.

Read and study Hebrews 11:1 (TLB).
What is faith? It is the confident assurance that something we want is going to happen. It is the certainty that what we hope for is waiting for us, even though we cannot see it up ahead.

Notes from the *Reformation Study* Bible
For the time being, only faith can see the future as it receives the promises of God.

Analyze:
What are the key points from Hebrews 11:1?

Summarize:
In your own words, explain Hebrews 11:1.

Read and study Hebrews 10:23 (TLB).
Now we can look forward to the salvation God has promised us. There is no longer any room for doubt, and we can tell others that salvation is ours, for there is no question that he will do what he says.

Notes from the *Reformation Study* Bible
The confession of our hope refers to the time of baptism as verse 22 refers to water.

Analyze:
What are the key points from Hebrews 10:23?

Summarize:
In your own words, explain Hebrews 10:23.

Read and study Ephesians 2:8.
For it is by grace you have been saved, through faith—
and this is not from yourselves, it is the gift of God.

Notes from the *Reformation Study* Bible
Salvation is a completed action that has a current effect. This is thought to be salvation by faith, which is a gift of God, while others think of it as plain "faith."

Analyze:
What are the key points from Ephesians 2:8?

Summarize:
In your own words, explain Ephesians 2:8.

Read and study 1 Corinthians 16:13.
>Be on your guard; stand firm in the faith; be courageous; be strong.

Notes from *Matthew Henry's Commentary*
Christians should always be on their guard since they are always in danger. This was the case of the Corinthian church with deceivers in their midst who were bent on corrupting their faith.

Analyze:
What are the key points from 1 Corinthians 16:13?

Summarize:
In your own words, explain 1 Corinthians 16:13.

Read and study Hebrews 11:6.
And without faith it is impossible to please God, because anyone who comes to him must believe that he exists and that he rewards those who earnestly seek him.

Notes from the *Reformation Study* Bible
Faith is a necessity to understand the things of God and to believe him and seek him.

Analyze:
What are the key points from Hebrews 11:6?

Summarize:
In your own words, explain Hebrews 11:6.

Respond:
Pick one scripture verse from the following: Hebrews 11:1, Hebrews 10:23, Ephesians 2:8, 1 Corinthians 16:13, and Hebrews 11:6, and in your own words, explain hope and/or faith and describe how this verse has helped you to utilize faith and/or hope in your life.

Obtain your spiritual breakthrough by standing on God's promises.

Read and study Psalm 145:13.
Your kingdom is an everlasting kingdom, and your dominion endures through all generations. The Lord is trustworthy in all he promises and faithful in all he does.

Notes from the *Reformation Study* Bible
God is eternal and his kingdom will never be destroyed. Refer to Dan. 4:34.

Analyze:
What are the key points from Psalm 145:13?

Summarize:
In your own words, explain Psalm 145:13.

Read and study Joshua 23:14.
> Now I am about to go the way of all the earth. You know with all your heart and soul that not one of all the good promises the Lord your God gave you has failed. Every promise has been fulfilled; not one has failed.

Notes from the *Reformation Study* Bible
Knowledge of God's faithfulness is not simply intellectual but shapes every aspect of a person's life.

Analyze:
What are the key points from Joshua 23:14?

Summarize:
In your own words, explain Joshua 23:14.

Respond:
What do Psalm 145:13 and Joshua 23:14 say about God and His promises? Give an example of how and when you stood on God's promises and the results that you obtained.

Week 18.

Accompanying Your Purpose in Life

- Describe your purpose even if you have not accomplished it.

- Discuss roadblocks you encountered—or will encounter—in getting to your purpose.

- Discuss how the process of experiencing stumbling blocks has increased your endurance and your faith.

Describe how you arrived or will arrive at accomplishing your purpose.

Discuss roadblocks you encountered—or will encounter—in getting to your purpose.

Discuss how the process of experiencing stumbling blocks has increased your endurance and your faith.

Week 19.

Maintaining Your Purpose

- Describe how you are maintaining your purpose in the following areas:
    - Describe how you schedule time to read God's Word, pray, praise, worship God, and listen to Him.
    - Describe how you are scheduling time to care for your body—God's temple—by eating the right foods, drinking water, and exercising at least three times per week. Why do you believe these steps are important?
    - Describe your monthly, quarterly or yearly retreat times that you schedule to be alone with God. How have you benefited from your times alone with God?

- Moving to the Next Level with God

- Explain that your purpose is to benefit others.

- Explain the following statement:
  "God orders your steps for His purposes and for his glory."

- Read, study, analyze, summarize, and respond to the following scripture verses to learn how God orders your steps for his purposes and for his glory:
    - Ephesians 4:7
    - Joshua 15:5
    - Job 12:13
    - Psalm 23:3

Describe how you are scheduling time to read God's Word, pray, praise, worship God, and listen to Him. Why do you believe listening to God is necessary?

Describe how you are scheduling time to care for your body—God's temple—by eating the right foods, drinking water, and exercising at least three times per week. Why do you believe these steps are important?

Describe your monthly, quarterly or yearly retreat times that you schedule to be alone with God. How have you benefited from your times alone with God?

Moving to the Next Level with God

Respond:
Explain fully why operating in your purpose benefits others by affecting changes in their lives. What changes have you observed in those to whom you have ministered?

Respond:
Explain the following statement:

"God orders your steps for His purposes and for His glory."

Read and study Ephesians 4:7 (NKJV).
But to each one of us grace was given according to the measure of Christ's gift.

Notes from the *Reformation Study* Bible
All Christians share the gift of salvation through faith. Others are given individual gifts to be used for the church. Apostle Paul talks about his own gift in Ephesians 3: 2, 8.

Analyze:
What are the key points from Ephesians 4:7?

Summarize:
In your own words, explain Ephesians 4:7.

Read and study John 15:5 (NKJV).

"I am the vine, you are the branches. He who abides in Me, and I in him, bears much fruit; for without Me you can do nothing."

Notes from the *Reformation Study* Bible

Saving grace is necessary for the beginning, the development and completion of the salvation process.

Analyze:
What are the key points from John 15:5?

Summarize:
In your own words, explain John 15:5.

Read and study Job 12:13 (NKJV).
"With Him are wisdom and strength,
He has counsel and understanding."

Notes from the *Reformation Study* Bible:
Job—in contrast to his counselors—talks *to* God in Job 13:20. Note the difference: his advisors spoke *of* God.

Analyze:
What are the key points from Job 12:13?

Summarize:
In your own words, explain Job 12:13.

Read and study Psalm 23:3 (NKJV).
"He restores my soul;
He leads me in the paths of righteousness
For His name's sake. "

Notes from the *Reformation Study* Bible
This explains how God as shepherd, cares for his sheep.

Analyze:
What are the key points from Psalm 23:3?

Summarize.
In your own words, explain Psalm 23:3.

Respond:
Explain what you have learned from the following scripture verses: Ephesians 4:7, Joshua 15:5, Job 12:3, and Psalm 23:3.

In what ways have these verses impacted your life?

Week 20.

Walking with God

- Understanding God's commandments and statutes
- Read, study, analyze, summarize, and respond to the following scripture verses to understand God's commandments and statutes:
    - Mark 10:19
    - Romans 13:9
    - Daniel 9:4
    - Deuteronomy 9:4-6
    - Exodus 15:25-26
    - Ezekiel 36:26-27

- Living in Obedience to God's Will

- Read, study, analyze, summarize, and respond to the following scripture verses to understand how to live in obedience to God's will:
    - Deuteronomy 5:33
    - 2 John 1:6

- Understanding Who Almighty God Is

- Read, study, analyze, summarize, and respond to the following scripture verses to understand who Almighty God is:
    - Revelation 16:7
    - 1 John 4:8
    - Micah 7:18
    - 1 Corinthians 1:9
    - 1 Corinthians 8:6

- Understanding Fully Who You Are in Christ

- Read, study, analyze, summarize, and respond to the following scripture verses to understand who you are in Christ:
    - Romans 8:17
    - Galatians 3:26
    - Colossians 2:10

- Fulfilling Your Destiny as An Ambassador for Christ on this Earth

- Definition of an Ambassador for Christ

- Read, study, analyze, summarize, and respond to the following scripture verses to understand your destiny as an ambassador for Christ:
    - Ephesians 6:20
    - 2 Corinthians 5:20

Understanding God's Commandments and Statutes

Read and study Mark 10:19 (NKJV).
You know the commandments: 'Do not commit adultery,' 'Do not murder,' 'Do not steal,' 'Do not bear false witness,' 'Do not defraud,' 'Honor your father and your mother.'

Notes from the *Reformation Study* Bible
This account gives true messages on messiahship and discipleship.

Analyze:
What are the key points from Mark 10:19?

Summarize:
In your own words, explain Mark 10:19.

Read and study Romans 13:9 (NKJV).
For the commandments, "You shall not commit adultery," "You shall not murder," "You shall not steal," You shall not bear false witness," "You shall not covet," and if there is any other commandment, are all summed up in this saying, namely, "You shall love your neighbor as yourself."

Notes from the *Reformation Study* Bible
You were created in the image of God and as such you should relate to others with that same love and not out of self-love.

Analyze:
What are the key points from Romans 13:9?

Summarize:
In your own words, explain Romans 13:9.

Read and study Daniel 9:4 (NKJV).
And I prayed to the Lord my God, and made confession, and said, "O Lord, great and awesome God, who keeps His covenant and mercy with those who love Him, and with those who keep His commandments."

Notes from the *Reformation Study* Bible
This prayer is rooted in the relationship of God to his people: blessings for obedience and curses for disobedience. Refer to Nehemiah 9 for a similar prayer.

Analyze:
What are the key points from Daniel 9:4?

Summarize:
In your own words, explain Daniel 9:4.

Read and study Deuteronomy 6:4-6.
Hear, O Israel: The Lord our God, the Lord is one. Love the Lord your God with all your heart and with all your soul and with all your strength. These commandments that I give you today are to be on your hearts.

Notes from the *Reformation Study* Bible:
The Lord is One affirms both God's uniqueness and unity or singularity—the only God is One. As the Old Testament implies and the New Testament teaches, there is differentiation of Persons within the Godhead—one and three. Refer to Isaiah 44:6.

Other Related Research
Deuteronomy 6:4-6 (called the *Sh'ma* in Hebrew from the Hebrew plural imperative for "Hear!") is both a pivotal prayer and concept in Judaism. It is recited daily by observant Jewish people. The *Sh'ma* is also directly or closely quoted in Luke 10:27, Matthew 22 and Mark 12.

Analyze:
What are the key points from Deuteronomy 6:4-6?

Summarize:
In your own words, explain Deuteronomy 6:4-6.

God's statutes include listening to God's voice; doing what God considers to be right; obeying his commandments to love God and keep his statutes.

Read and study Exodus 15:25-26.
Then Moses cried out to the Lord, and the Lord showed him a piece of wood. He threw it into the water, and the water became fit to drink. There the Lord issued a ruling and instruction for them and put them to the test. He said, "If you listen carefully to the Lord your God and do what is right in his eyes, if you pay attention to his commands and keep all his decrees, I will not bring on you any of the diseases I brought on the Egyptians, for I am the Lord, who heals you. "

Notes from the *Reformation Study* Bible
The general term for God's law (Torah) is the form of the verb (showed). God's revelation is a statute and a rule. God's Word instructs Israel as he leads and proves them. God has the power and the mercy to heal (Deut 32:39; Psalm 103:3).

Analyze:
What are the key points from Exodus 15: 25-26?

Summarize:
In your own words, explain Exodus 15: 25-26.

Read and study Ezekiel 36:26-27.
I will give you a new heart and put a new spirit in you; I will remove from you your heart of stone and give you a heart of flesh. And I will put my Spirit in you and move you to follow my decrees and be careful to keep my laws.

Notes from the *Reformation Study* Bible
God will remove a heart of stone and put a heart of flesh not by human attainment but by God's divine initiative so that one will respond to God by being obedient.

Analyze:
What are the key points from Ezekiel 36:26-27?

Summarize:
In your own words, explain Ezekiel 36:26-27.

Using two or more scripture references from the list below, explain God's commandments and statutes and why you should observe them.
- Mark 10:19
- Romans 13:9
- Daniel 9:4
- Deuteronomy 9:4-6
- Exodus 15:25-26
- Ezekiel 36:26-27

If you are not observing them, what steps you must take in your life to be in line with God's commandments and statutes?

Living in Obedience to God's Will

Read and study Deuteronomy 5:33.
Walk in obedience to all that the Lord your God has commanded you, so that you may live and prosper and prolong your days in the land that you will possess.

Notes from the *Reformation Study* Bible
Moses expounds the way of life in the covenant.

Analyze:
What are the key points from Deuteronomy 5:33?

Summarize:
In your own words, explain Deuteronomy 5:33.

Read and study 2 John 1:6 (NKJV).
This is love, that we walk according to His commandments. This is the commandment, that as you have heard from the beginning, you should walk in it.

Notes from the *Reformation Study* Bible
The mark of Christian faithfulness is love for one another, the command that Jesus gave himself in John 13:34.

Analyze:
What are the key points from 2 John 1:6?

Summarize:
In your own words, explain 2 John 1:6.

Respond:
From the above scriptures what does God require of you?

Understanding Who Almighty God Is

Read and study Revelation 16:7 (TLB).
And I heard the angel of the altar say, "Yes, Lord God Almighty, your punishments are just and true."

Notes from the *Reformation Study* Bible
This is the report of the seven angels who received the command to pour out the seven bowls of God's wrath upon the earth. Refer to Jeremiah 25:15-29 and Ezekiel 23:31-34. The bowls are poured out at God's command in Rev. 16:1 leading to the seven last plagues and to the second coming of Christ. The bowls represent judgements against evil doers.

Analyze:
What are the key points from Revelation 16:7?

Summarize:
In your own words, explain Revelation 16:7.

Read and study 1 John 4:8.
   Whoever does not love does not know God, because God is love.

Notes from the *Reformation Study* Bible
The love of God, the Father for his only Son is the source of love that binds the fellowship of believers as a family.

Analyze:
What are the key points from 1 John 4:8?

Summarize:
In your own words, explain 1 John 4:8.

Read and study Micah 7:18 (TLB).
Where is another God like you, who pardons the sins of the survivors among his people? You cannot stay angry with your people, for you love to be merciful.

Notes from the *Reformation Study* Bible
Micah's name means "Who is like the Lord." Here, he emphasizes God's pardoning grace.

Analyze:
What are the key points from Micah 7:18?

Summarize:
In your own words, explain Micah 7:18.

Read and study 1 Corinthians 1:9 (TLB).
God will surely do this for you, for he always does just what he says, and he is the one who invited you into this wonderful friendship with his Son, even Christ our Lord.

Notes from *Matthew Henry's Commentary*
He who has begun a good work in you would not leave it unfinished. Those that wait for the coming of our Lord Jesus Christ will be kept by him and confirmed to the end; and those that are so, will be blameless in the day of Christ.

Analyze:
What are the key points from 1 Corinthians 1:9?

Summarize:
In your own words, explain 1 Corinthians 1:9.

Read and study 1 Corinthians 8:6 (TLB).
> But we know that there is only one God, the Father, who created all things and made us to be his own; and one Lord Jesus Christ, who made everything and gives us life.

Notes from *Matthew Henry's Commentary*
Gods of the Heathens are not God; they are false gods.
"The heathens had many such gods, some in heaven and some on earth, celestial deities, that were of highest rank and repute among them, and terrestrial ones, men made into gods, that were to mediate for men with the former, and were deputed by them to preside over earthly affairs. These are in scripture commonly called Baalim. There is only one God, and the Mediator between God and man, Jesus Christ. God is the fountain of being, the author of all things, maker, preserver and governor of the whole world, of whom and by whom are all things."

Analyze:
What are the key points from 1 Corinthians 8:6?

Summarize:
In your own words, explain 1 Corinthians 8:6.

Respond:
From your research, your study of the scripture verses, based on who God is, and from your own experiences with Him, explain in your own words how God has impacted your life.

Understanding Fully Who You Are in Christ

Read and study Romans 8:17 (TLB).
And since we are his children, we will share his treasures—for all God gives to his Son Jesus is now ours too. But if we are to share his glory, we must also share his suffering.

Notes from the *Reformation Study* Bible
Just as the children of a family share in the inheritance of their father, so we as God's children are heirs just as Christ is. That involves sharing in his suffering.

Analyze:
What are the key points from Romans 8:17?

Summarize:
In your own words, explain Romans 8:17.

Read and study Galatians 3:26.
So, in Christ Jesus you are all children of God through faith.

Notes from the *Reformation Study* Bible
We are adopted sons/daughters because we are united to the true Son, Jesus Christ. Baptism seals that union with Christ. To be clothed with Christ implies Christ lives in us and Christ died and lives for us. Christ is our covering, and we are a new creation in Christ (Rom. 13:14; Eph.4:24; Col.3:10).

Analyze:
What are the key points from Galatians 3:26?

Summarize:
In your own words, explain Galatians 3:26.

Read and study Colossians 2:10 (TLB).
So you have everything when you have Christ, and you are filled with God through your union with Christ. He is the highest Ruler, with authority over every other power.

Notes from the *Reformation Study* Bible
The fullness of God abides in Christ and is obtained only through him. See Colossians 1:19-20.

Analyze:
What are the key points from Colossians 2:10?

Summarize:
In your own words, explain Colossians 2:10.

Respond:
What does it mean to be complete in Christ as referenced by Colossians 2:10?

How does this scripture verse help you solve areas in your life where you had doubts concerning your ability to cope and/or overcome your difficulties?

Fulfilling Your Destiny as An Ambassador for Christ on this Earth (at Church, Home, Work or Wherever You Go)

Definition:
The *Collins English Dictionary* defines an ambassador as an important official who lives in a foreign country and represents his or her own country's interests there.

As Christians, we are diplomats sent by God to represent him in foreign countries if we chose to go there, at home, at church or synagogue, at our workplaces, through our volunteer efforts or in our communities.

Read and study Ephesians 6:20 (TLB).
I am in chains now for preaching this message from God. But pray that I will keep on speaking out boldly for him even here in prison, as I should.

Notes from the *Reformation Study* Bible
This is a call for prayer on behalf of all believers as well as for Paul himself. See Ephesians 1:15-23.

Analyze:
What are the key points from Ephesians 6:20?

Summarize:
In your own words, explain Ephesians 6:20.

Read and study 2 Corinthians 5:20 (TLB).
> We are Christ's ambassadors. God is using us to speak to you: we beg you, as though Christ himself were here pleading with you, receive the love he offers you—be reconciled to God.

Notes from the *Reformation Study* Bible
While Paul is appealing directly to the Corinthians "to be reconciled to God," he is appealing to the world to be reconciled. Reconciliation is restoring of loving fellowship. For Christians, we are reconciled to God each day. See Matt. 6:12; 1 John 1:9.

Analyze:
What are the key points from 2 Corinthians 5:20?

Summarize:
Explain how Apostle Paul used his position as an ambassador to speak to the Ephesian and Corinthian Churches.

Respond:
Have you worked as an Ambassador for Christ?

If you haven't, what plans are you making in the future to do so?

How do you plan to effect changes in the lives of others for God's glory?

About the Author

Joan M. Blake is a motivational speaker and spiritual life-coach. She is the author of seven inspirational books, including, Standing on His Promises: Finding Comfort, Hope, and Purpose in the Midst of Your Storm, published by Key to Life Publishing Company. She conducts women's retreats, workshops dealing with life issues for parents and teens, and writes a blog at keytolifeblog.com.

She is the founder and president of Christian Resource Network, Inc., a non-profit organization providing support to youth and families at christianresourcenetwork.org.

She and her husband, Carl, live in the Boston area, and are the parents of two sons and two daughters and have several grandchildren.

Other Books Written by the Author:

Standing on His Promises:
Finding Comfort, Hope, and Purpose in the Midst of Your Storm

Prayer and Meditation:
Finding Comfort, Hope, and Purpose in the Midst of Your Storm

Prayer and Meditation for Teens:
Finding Comfort, Hope, and Purpose in the Midst of Your Storm

Prayer and Meditation:
Biblical Self-Help Tools for Parents of Teens when You Do Not Know where to Turn

Rise Up:
How to Overcome Your Battles Utilizing Faith and Belief in God

Gentle Breeze:
Finding Comfort, Hope, and Purpose in the Midst of Your Storm

Prayers on the Go: Finding Peace in Difficult Times

Contact us! We'd love to hear from you:

WEB	keytolifepublishingcompany.com
	Keytolifeblog.com
EMAIL	admin@keytolifepublishingcompany.com
	joan@keytolifeblog.com

KEY TO LIFE PUBLISHING COMPANY
P.O. Box 190971 • Boston, MA 02119

Like us on Facebook:
Facebook.com/keytolifepublishingcompany

Follow me on Twitter:
Twitter.com/@JoanMBlake

Follow us on Instagram:
Keytolifepublishingcompany.com

www.ingramcontent.com/pod-product-compliance
Lightning Source LLC
Chambersburg PA
CBHW030444300426
44112CB00009B/1158